S0-BCO-897

DRAWING FANTASY MONSTERS

ILLUSTRATED BY JANOS JANTNER

PowerKiDS
press™

New York

Published in 2013 by The Rosen Publishing Group, Inc.
29 East 21st Street, New York, NY 10010

First Edition

Produced for Rosen by Calcium Creative Ltd
Editors: Sarah Eason and Rosie Hankin
Editor for Rosen: Sara Antill
Book Design: Paul Myerscough

Illustrations by Janos Jantner

Library of Congress Cataloging-in-Publication Data

Jantner, Janos.
 Drawing fantasy monsters / by Janos Jantner. — 1st ed.
     p. cm. — (How to draw monsters)
 Includes index.
 ISBN 978-1-4777-0311-3 (library binding) —
 ISBN 978-1-4777-0344-1 (pbk.) — ISBN 978-1-4777-0345-8 (6-pack)
 1. Fantasy in art—Juvenile literature. 2. Monsters in art—Juvenile literature.
 3. Drawing—Technique—Juvenile literature. I. Title.
 NC825.F25J36 2013
 743'.87—dc23
                                                            2012026859

Manufactured in the United States of America

CPSIA Compliance Information: Batch #W13PK7: For Further Information contact Rosen Publishing, New York, New York at 1-800-237-9932

CONTENTS

FANTASY MONSTERS

From towering giants, dragons, and humanlike beasts called orcs and elves, through evil witches and wizards casting dangerous spells, people love to be scared by fantasy monsters! Now you can bring your very own terrifying monsters to life through art!

YOU WILL NEED

Just a few simple pieces of equipment are needed to create awesome monster drawings:

Sketchpad or paper
Visit an art store to buy good quality paper.

Pencils
A range of drawing pencils are essential. You will need both fine-tipped and thick-tipped pencils.

Eraser
You can remove any unwanted lines with an eraser, and you can even use it to add highlights.

Paintbrush, paints, and pens
Buy a set of quality paints, brushes, and coloring pens to add color to your monster drawings.

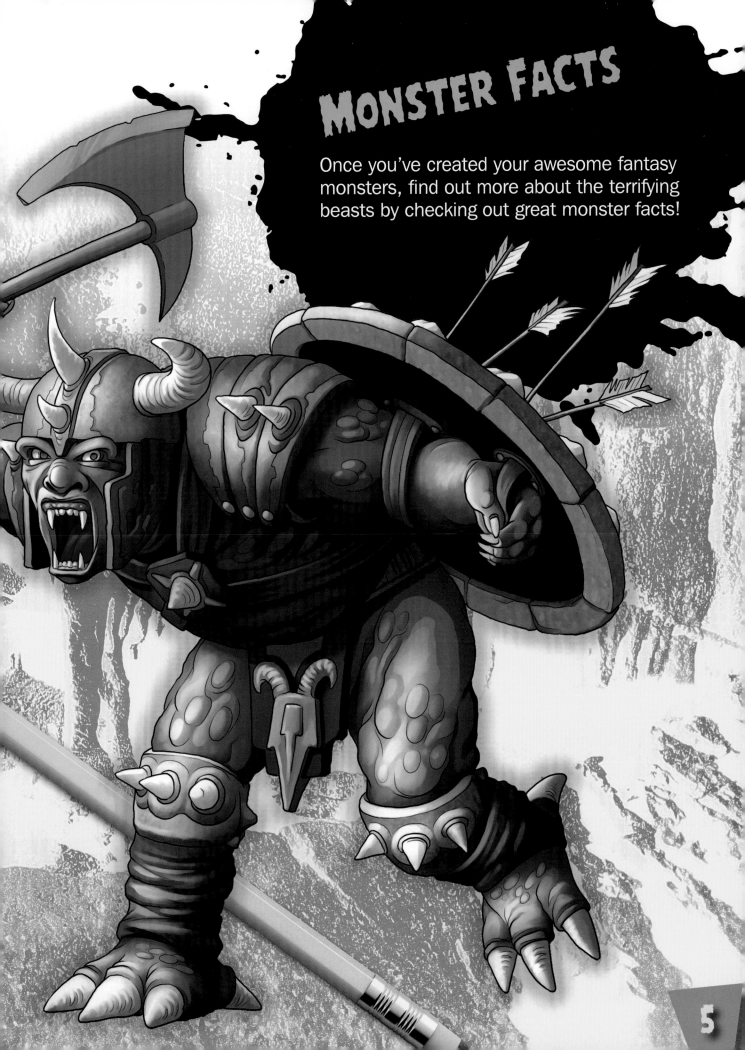

MONSTER FACTS

Once you've created your awesome fantasy monsters, find out more about the terrifying beasts by checking out great monster facts!

WICKED GIANT

or thousands of years, tales have been told of big, bulky creatures called giants. These huge beasts look like human beings, yet they are amazingly tall and very strong. Some giants are gentle, but others are said to destroy anything in their path. Beware!

STEP 1

Use rectangles and ovals to draw the head, trunk, arms, legs, hands, and feet. Draw the monster as if it is lunging toward you.

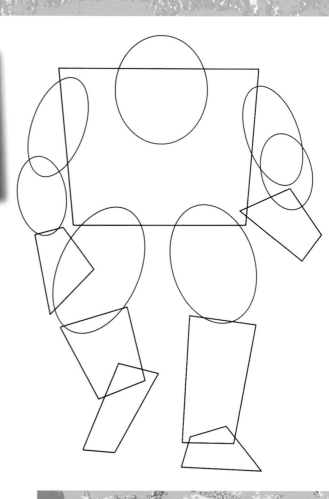

STEP 2

Draw over your shapes to create the giant's outline. Erase the shapes you drew in step 1. Begin to draw the features of the face. Then add the boots and a shirt.

STEP 3

Now you can begin to add more detail. Pencil lines to show the giant's hair and bristly beard. Draw its wide nose and add some wrinkles around the face. Then add a tight belt around its bulging belly. Add fingernails to your giant's enormous hands and some knobbly knees to its legs. This giant is huge and clumsy!

STEP 4

Add some blunt and broken teeth to the gaping jaw. Use a fine-tipped pencil to draw more strands of hair, and add some piercing eyes. Draw buttons on the giant's shirt and cuffs. Then add some creases to its clothes.

Add some shading to your monster's face. Concentrate on the brow, cheeks, and chin. Then shade the monster's wide mouth to show off its jagged teeth! Add shading to the jacket, waist, hands, and boots.

STEP 6

Begin to color your giant. Use a palette of pink and brown for the skin. Use shades of brown for the belt, boots, and pants. Then use green for the shirt. Don't forget the hair!

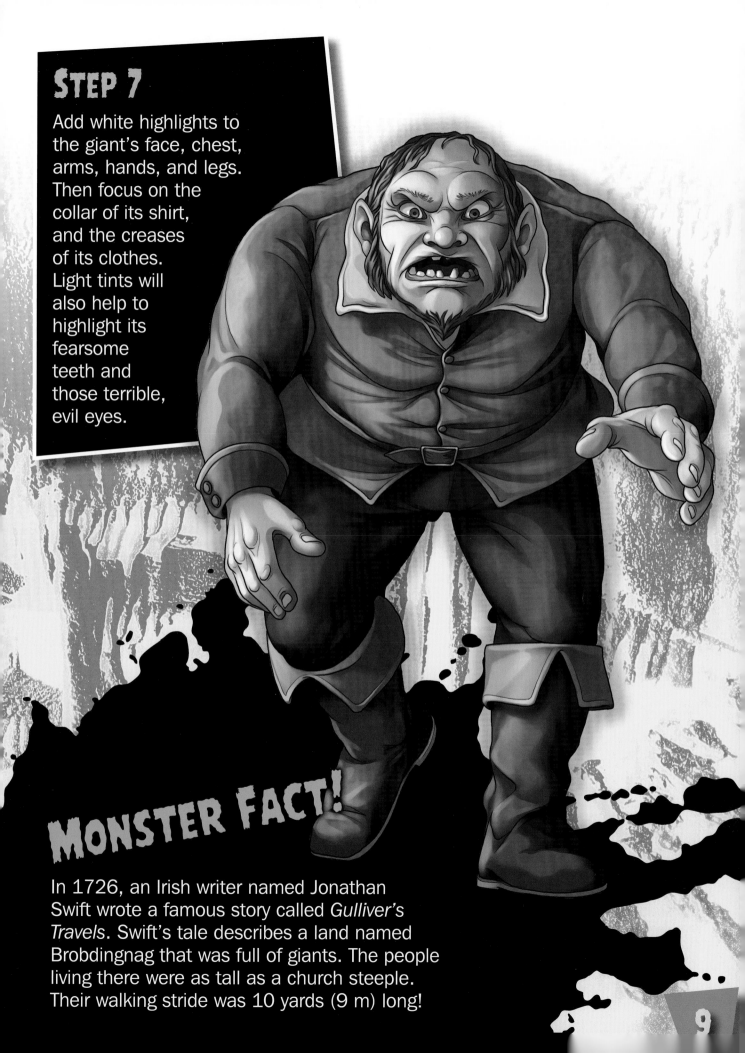

STEP 7

Add white highlights to the giant's face, chest, arms, hands, and legs. Then focus on the collar of its shirt, and the creases of its clothes. Light tints will also help to highlight its fearsome teeth and those terrible, evil eyes.

MONSTER FACT!

In 1726, an Irish writer named Jonathan Swift wrote a famous story called *Gulliver's Travels*. Swift's tale describes a land named Brobdingnag that was full of giants. The people living there were as tall as a church steeple. Their walking stride was 10 yards (9 m) long!

9

EVIL WIZARD

In myths and legends, wizards have been casting spells for hundreds of years. Known for their special magical powers, wizards are sometimes described as wise old men. They often wear a cloak and a tall, pointed hat. Evil wizards wear a dark-colored cloak, and their dangerous spells are called "black magic."

STEP 1

To create your wizard, draw ovals for his head and arms. Then draw rectangles and triangles for his cloak, body, and long boots.

STEP 2

Draw a fine line over the outline and erase your rough shapes from step 1. Draw your wizard's face and fingers.

STEP 3

Now you can add more detail to your drawing. Draw the strands of your wizard's bushy eyebrows and his long, flowing beard. Draw a rope tied around his cloak, with two tassels. Then draw a long staff in his right hand. Notice the magical crystal at the top of the staff, tightly clapsed by a clawed, metal hand.

STEP 4

Use a fine-tipped pencil to add pupils to the eyes. Then use fine strokes to give the beard a soft, shaggy feel. Draw the knot of the belt, the strands of the tassels, and the clothes' creases.

Add shading to the inside of the cloak's hood and sleeves. Then shade parts of the face, beard, and boots. Shading will add a 3D effect to your drawing. Now your wizard is coming to life!

STEP 6

Put a wash of dark blue over the cloak. Then use a palette of pink and brown for the skin. Use white and gray for the hair and beard. Then use shades of brown for the belt, boots, and staff.

STEP 7

Give your wizard's magical crystal a glow, using white highlights and a hint of green. Then add white tints to the creases of the clothes and the strands of thick, flowing hair. Don't forget to highlight your wizard's piercing, brown eyes.

MONSTER FACT!

The name "wizard" comes from the old English word "wys," meaning "wise." Not all wizards are evil. In some stories, wizards are kind and use their spells to help other people. These wizards are said to practice "white magic."

AWESOME ORC

At first sight, this fierce creature is like a human being. But if you look closely, you can see strange features such as pointed ears or gray-green skin. Orcs are smaller than a person, but they can be very strong. With their sharp teeth, they are also known to like the taste of human flesh!

STEP 1

Draw ovals to create your orc's head, arms, legs, and shield. Then use rectangles for the trunk and the lower part of the legs.

STEP 2

Pencil the monster's outline, then erase the shape lines from step 1. Draw an ax in the orc's right hand, and a horned helmet.

STEP 3

Now add spikes to the orc's armor. This is worn to protect the shoulders, chest, groin, wrists, and knees. Draw the fingers and also add some nails. Then draw four razor-sharp claws on each foot. Don't forget to add detail to the shield strapped to the orc's left arm.

STEP 4

Use a fine-tipped pencil to fill the orc's gaping jaw with some terrible teeth. Add some muscles and bulges to its tough, leathery skin. Add some detail to its armor. Then draw the four feathered arrows in its shield.

15

STEP 5

It's time to bring your orc to life with some 3D effects. Use shading to give your drawing depth. Then shade the shield's underside, the inside of the orc's mighty mouth, and parts of its neck, arms, waist, and legs.

STEP 6

Use a palette of brown, gray, and green to add color to your drawing. Use gray for the cold, sharp steel of the armor and ax. Use red for the gums and tongue, and ivory for the teeth and nails.

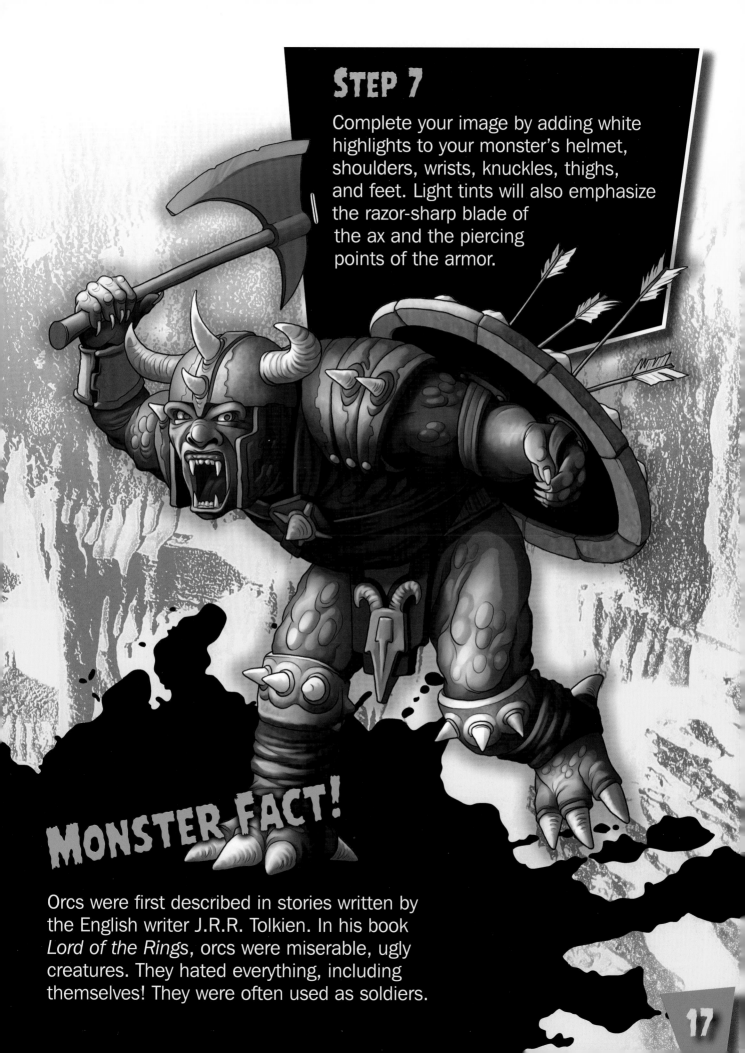

Complete your image by adding white highlights to your monster's helmet, shoulders, wrists, knuckles, thighs, and feet. Light tints will also emphasize the razor-sharp blade of the ax and the piercing points of the armor.

MONSTER FACT!

Orcs were first described in stories written by the English writer J.R.R. Tolkien. In his book *Lord of the Rings*, orcs were miserable, ugly creatures. They hated everything, including themselves! They were often used as soldiers.

DEADLY DRAGON

This scary creature has a body like a lizard or a snake. It has scaly skin, terrible teeth, and sharp claws. Some dragons have very powerful wings and can breathe fire. Dragons eat anything! They have been described as one of Earth's most dangerous creatures.

STEP 1

Draw triangles, rectangles, and ovals for your dragon's wings, feet, legs, and head. Then draw a curve for its neck, body, and tail.

STEP 2

Draw a finer pencil outline and erase the lines made in step 1. Begin to add the features of the face and the clawed feet.

STEP 3

Now add some detail to your drawing. Draw sharp spines along your beast's back, from the top of the head to the tip of the tail. Add some razor-sharp claws to the toes. Then draw a straggly beard on the chin. Don't forget to draw the barbels on the dragon's cheeks and head.

STEP 4

Use a fine-tipped pencil to fill the dragon's mouth with flesh-tearing teeth. Add pupils to the piercing eyes. Then draw the bones and ridges of the wings.

Now shade your picture to add more depth. Shade parts of the dragon's face, neck, legs, and belly. Begin to draw the detail of its tough, scaly skin.

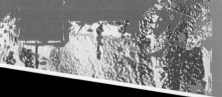

STEP 6

Bring your dragon to life with a wash of blue-gray. Use light shades for the wings, snout, and belly. Then use darker shades for the head, neck, back, and tail. Use dark gray for the tough spines and the tip of the tail. Don't forget to color the sharp claws.

STEP 7

Now for some finishing touches. Add highlights to your beast's body. This will show how big and bulky it is. Light tints will highlight the roundness of the belly and the curve of the tail. Light tints will also show the delicate wings and the sharp edges of the spines and claws. Finally, give your dragon an evil glint in its eyes.

MONSTER FACT!

In the West, dragons are said to be fierce and evil. But in the East, dragons are described as gentle and wise. They are thought to bring good luck. Many temples have been built to worship Eastern dragons.

SORCERESS

A sorceress is a type of witch. She uses her magical powers to make evil spells. This dark magic causes harm to other people, objects, or animals. A sorceress is said to worship the devil. She often wears a pointed hat. Stories tell of sorceresses flying through the sky on broomsticks!

STEP 1

Use a mixture of ovals, triangles, and rectangles to draw your sorceress's head, body, clothes, and pointed hat.

STEP 2

Pencil the sorceress's outline, then erase the lines from step 1. Draw the face, hair, and hands. Then add detail to the dress.

STEP 3

Focus on the features of the face. Notice how your sorceress has a scary smile. Draw her long strands of hair, the waist of her dress, and some sharp fingernails. Draw a staff in her right hand. Leave space for the magical crystal.

STEP 4

Now add more detail to your drawing. Add pupils to the eyes, ties to the bodice, wrinkles to the skin, and creases to the clothes. Show the staff's crystal within in the metal swirl.

Now shade the inside of the draping sleeves and parts of the hat. Shade the creases of the clothes and areas of the face and neck. Shading will add depth to your drawing.

STEP 6

Use a wash of purple to color your sorceress's clothes and her pointed hat. Then use a palette of pink and brown for her skin. Give the magical crystal a purple sheen. Then use a dark shade of gray for the hair, eyes, and fingernails.

STEP 7

Finally, add some white highlights to the sorceress's skin to bring her body to life. Light tints on the creases of the clothes will also give your picture more depth. Use tints on the bodice ties to emphasize the waist. Then give the magical crystal an strange glow. Watch out, she's about to cast an evil spell!

MONSTER FACT!

The name "sorceress" comes from the Latin word "*sortiariusm*," which means "someone who can see or change the future." Long ago, a sorceress was often blamed for bad things that happened in a local community.

DARK ELF

These cruel creatures live underground. They look like humans and are similar to dwarves. Dark elves hate sunlight. In fact, they turn to stone if they see the Sun! They live in dark places and love to lurk in shadows. Dark elves cheat and lie. They are greedy creatures and are always ready to pick a fight.

STEP 1

Use a mixture of ovals and rectangles to draw your dark elf's head, trunk, arms, legs, hands, and feet.

STEP 2

Pencil the elf's outline, then erase the lines from step 1. Begin to draw the features of the face, hair, and clothes.

STEP 3

Now draw lines to show the straggly strands of hair, the ribs, and parts of the elf's armor. This is worn to protect the shoulders, chest, elbows, waist, and knees. Draw the outline of the long boots and the arm sleeves.

STEP 4

Use a fine-tipped pencil to add more detail to your drawing. Add pupils to the eyes and more strands to the hair. Draw the ridges of the pointed ears, and add more detail to the clothes. Then draw a sharp sword held tightly in the elf's right hand.

STEP 5

Add some shading to give your elf a 3D effect. Shade the heavy brow, the hollows of the cheeks, and the eye sockets. Then add shading to the neck, waist, arms, legs, and the body armor.

STEP 6

Use a palette of pink, brown, and gray to bring your dark elf to life. Use gray for the long hair and the shiny sword. Add some piercing brown eyes. Then use shades of brown to give the armor some texture.

STEP 7

Now add some white highlights to give your drawing more depth and drama. Use light tints to show the sharp, shiny blade. Highlights will help to show the surfaces of the skin and the smooth curves of the armor. Use tints to give the hair a soft sheen. Then add a scary glint to the evil eyes.

MONSTER FACT!

Snorri Sturluson was a historian who lived in Iceland around 800 years ago. He wrote about dark elves in his books about myths and legends. He said that dark elves were the opposite of "light elves," which were said to live in heaven.

GLOSSARY

armor (AR-mer) Metal coverings worn in battle.

barbels (BAR-belz) Whisker-like features on sea creatures.

bodice (BOD-is) Part of a dress, found above the waist.

brow (BROW) A ridge over the eyes.

bulky (BULK-ee) Heavily built and taking up a lot of space.

casting (KAST-ing) Making a spell or a trick work.

cloak (KLOHK) A type of robe that covers a person's body.

community (kuh-MYOO-nih-tee) The area in which a group of people live.

destroy (dih-STROY) To damage something beyond repair.

detail (dih-TAYL) The fine pencil markings on a drawing.

devil (DEH-vul) The ruler of evil.

drama (DRAH-muh) Excitement and exciting events.

features (FEE-churz) Particular parts of the face or body.

groin (GROYN) The area between the stomach and the thighs.

highlights (HY-lytz) Light parts.

historian (hih-STOR-ee-un) A person who studies history.

lunging (LUHN-jing) Making a sudden move forward.

miserable (MIH-zer-uh-bul) Very unhappy or uncomfortable.

myths (MITHS) Very old stories.

palette (PA-lit) A range of colors.

shading (SHAYD-ing) Pencil lines that add depth to a picture.

shadows (SHA-dohz) Dark areas where sunlight cannot reach.

soldiers (SOHL-jurz) People who fight in an army in times of war.

spells (SPEHLZ) Words or potions believed to have magical powers.

staff (STAF) A long wooden stick used for casting spells.

steeple (STEE-pul) The spire on top of a church tower or roof.

stride (STRYD) The length of one walking step.

temple (TEM-pel) A building used to worship a god or other spiritual being.

witch (WICH) A woman thought to have magical powers.

worship (WUR-shup) To show love to a god or other spiritual being.

FURTHER READING

Bergin, Mark. *How to Draw Fantasy Art*. How to Draw. New York: PowerKids Press, 2011.

Berry, Bob. *How to Draw Magical, Monstrous & Mythological Creatures*. Irvine, CA: Walter Foster Publishing, 2012.

Gray, Peter. *Everyone Can Draw Fantasy Figures*. Everyone Can Draw. New York: Windmill Books, 2013.

WEBSITES

Due to the changing nature of Internet links, PowerKids Press has developed an online list of websites related to the subject of this book. This site is updated regularly. Please use this link to access the list: www.powerkidslinks.com/htdm/fanta/

INDEX